lots of love

it's
a
girl
thing

Big hearts and sparkly tiaras to...

All the totes amazing Pink Ladies who read the books, visit the
website and message and mail both Lola and I – WE HEART YOU!

Angel boy Burt – love you x

Carrie and Jacqui, The girls from Shampoo – for being the most
fabulous inspir-o girls in my teendom years – Viva La Megababes!

Mrs Mclaren and Mr Clarke – the best teachers. Ever.

Susie and Izzi – so, we didn't rule the school? Pah! Look at us now – we rock n' rule!

Just Seventeen magazine for teaching me everything 'bout the big P when I was a teen girl.

Claire-bear Boxall and Clairey Brown-Smith for making life as an awkward teen girl in the world
totally do-able with fbs, photo swaps, phat mail and pages and pages of boyband chatter. Happy days.

Take That - the absolute best reason for being a teen girl in the 90s. Fact.

First published in the UK by HarperCollins Children's Books in 2008

1 3 5 7 9 10 8 6 4 2

ISBN-10: 0-00-726490-9

ISBN-13: 978-0-00-726490-2

A CIP catalogue record for this title is available from the British Library.

www.harpercollinschildrensbooks.co.uk

Text © 2008 Lisa Clark

Art © HarperCollins Children's Books

Art by Holly Lloyd

Printed and bound in China

Lola Love
it's a girl thing

By
Lisa Clark

HarperCollins *Children's Books*

Introduction

Being a girl in the world can be tough stuff, chica. Fact.

One minute you're brushing your Barbie doll's hair, the next you're diggin' on the totally cute guitar-playin' dude in the year above. Sigh.

That's not all, both your body and mind go through some pretty dramatic changes at a helluva crazy speed too. This, sweet thing, is your puberty makeover.

Now, I heart a makeover as much as the next chica, but ladybumps, mood-swings, hair sprouting here and there and periods? Well, there ain't no denying that they can be a complete head-mess. Whether your big P makeover is exciting, embarrassing, irritating or anxiety-inducing, don't freak out, the Pink Ladies and I have everything you need to make it as stress-free as possible. How?

Well, punk princess and Pink Lady Bella, who is a whole lot older than us, she's 17 which is like, practically a grown up – has completed her big P makeover and is the coolest mix of agony aunt, big sister and glossy girl 'zine in a rockgirl package. She's got the puberty 101 and together, 'coz yep, we're feeling it too sister, we'll make sure you're totally clued up about the whole big P makeover; it is a girl thing after all!

Love and pink lemonade bubbles,

Lola
xx

Your 'It's a girl thing!' bag of fabulousness

There's no right or wrong way to go through this whole puberty lark, however, armed with your 'It's a girl thing!' bag of fabulousness, it will inevitably be a whole lot less stressy, promise!

Peppermint tea – soothing, relieves bloating, caffeine-free and the perfect chill out tonic – ahhh.

Pampering treats – Because soaking in a bath not only makes you feel and look fabulous, sweet smelling products banish bad body odour too – yay!

Chocolate – well, why not?

Pink leg warmers – to wear while taking a brisk walk to the shop – exercise will make your body's natural pain killers kick-in if you've got bad belly pains.

Pink fluffy hot water bottle – If you can't bear to leave the sofa, sitting with a hot water bottle on your tum can work wonders and is really rather cute too.

checklist

So, what do you know?

Don't stress if you don't know exactly what's going on, you most deffo won't be the first girl in history to find puberty something right out of Scaryville, I know I did! Neither will you be the first to lie awake at night fretting that you're the only girl in class that doesn't wear a bra yet, just ask Pink Lady, Sadie... The trick is to Think Pink. Why?

Because Pink-Thinkin' chicks get clued-up about their bodies and what's going on inside. It's a fact that the more you know, the less confusing, surprising and embarrasing this whole hazy, crazy growing up stuff will seem! Ready?

Your boobs can be tender, sore and itchy during puberty

True ☑   or   False ☑

To get rid of body odour you should keep yourself clean and wash under your arms every day

True ☑   False ☑

Any hair that you shave will grow back much thicker

True ☑   False ☑

No two boobs are alike

True ☑   False ☑

Boys are just as self-conscious during puberty as girls

True ☑   False ☑

If you answered 'true' to 3 or more of the statements above...
You are sussed, sista! You know how puberty's body makeover will affect you and you're ready for action – go girl!

If you answered 'false' to 3 or more of the statements above...
No worries sweet thing, the Pink Ladies and I are gonna fill you in on everything from periods to ladybumps, because when you know what's happening to your body and why, you'll be much less likely to fret about it in the future, okay?

Ch-Ch-Ch-Changes

As you know I'm a pink-thinking chica on a daily basis and while I dig who I am and know I'm no ugly duckling, there are still times, even with all the pink thinking in the world, when I feel like one.
Sound familiar?

Blame the hormones.

Hormones are the chemicals your body produces to transform your sweet self from a young girl to a woman. These body changes can take years to unfold and take hold – yawn – and while there will deffo be some changes you'll like, there's a chance there will also be some that you won't.

Yes, this is rude and wrong, but unfortunately, chica, it is factuality.

If, like me, you're feeling a li'l bit messy and stressy about all this big P stuff, then hold up, because Bella is our 'big P go-to' about all things girl. She is the tiara-wearing princess of the bod squad – that's us btw – and together, we'll be answering all the need-to-know questions that you're too scared or embarrassed to ask – for the record though, NO question is ever too silly – I mean, how's a girl ever to become the most feisty, fun, fearless and fabulous girl in all of girlsville if she doesn't ask questions, eh?

la Bird Squad ladeees

What's happening?

So, Bella, what exactly is puberty anyway?

"...GIRLS, GIRLS, GIRLS... CHILL YOUR BOOTS — OR WHATEVER FOOTWEAR YOU'RE CURRENTLY WORKING — THIS PUBERTY LARK SEEMS MUCH BIGGER AND SCARIER THAN IT ACTUALLY IS.

HONEST.

IN FACT, ONCE YOU REALISE WHAT'S GOING ON, IT'S ACTUALLY A FUNNY KIND OF EXCITING. LET ME EXPLAIN... BASICALLY, PUBERTY IS WHEN YOUR BODY GETS A SERIOUS UPGRADE IN PREPARATION FOR BECOMING A WOMAN. COOL EH? YOU DEVELOP LADYBUMPS, YOUR HIPS BECOME WIDER AND YOU START YOUR PERIODS (MENSTRUAL CYCLE). WHILE ALL THIS IS GOING ON, YOUR HORMONES CAN ACT ALL KINDS OF CRAZY, WHICH CAN LEAVE YOU FEELING HAPPY, SAD, TEARFUL AND ANXIOUS ALL AT THE SAME TIME.

NOT SO COOL.

NOW, ALTHOUGH THE CHANGES THAT ARE HAPPENING TO YOUR BODY MAY SEEM SUPER SCARY, IT'S ALL COMPLETELY NORMAL, I PROMISE. I WAS FREAKED WHEN I SHOT UP TO GIRAFFE GIRL HEIGHT OVERNIGHT BUT THEN HAD TO WAIT FOR WHAT FELT LIKE FOREVER FOR SOMETHING, ANYTHING, THAT RESEMBLED BOOBS TO APPEAR.

Y'SEE, YOUR BIG P MAKEOVER IS TOTALLY UNIQUE TO YOU AND CAN KICK IN AT ANY TIME BETWEEN THE AGES OF EIGHT AND SEVENTEEN. THE GOOD NEWS IS THAT EVERYONE GOES THROUGH IT, JUST NOT NECESSARILY AT THE SAME TIME. SO DON'T PANIC IF YOUR GAL PALS START DEVELOPING BEFORE YOU — IT'S NOT A RACE, Y'KNOW!..."

Why does my mood flip from happy to sad without warning?
Are you on top of the world in the morning, depressed over lunch and angry in the evening? It's those pesky hormones again!

Science bit: Any changes in the level of oestrogen and progesterone hormones (these are the hormones you produce to keep your periods in check), can cause major irritability and mood swings and make you feel like you're riding an out-of-control rollercoaster.

Bod squad tip: Pink-thinkin' girls have a mood switch, something that will flick those dullsville clouds outta the sky and replace them with sunshine and sparkles! Lola keeps a journal to help her clear her messy, stressy head, I play guitar 'til my fingers are sore, Sadie creates a DIY craft-girl sensation with needle and thread and Angel will devour a glossy magazine from cover to cover.

What's your mood switch?
Make a list of all the things that will turn your frown upside down, and keep it nearby for the next time your mood takes a nosedive!

....

....

....

....

....

....

....

....

....

I spend ages looking at myself in the mirror and comparing myself to my mates. Is this normal?

Of course it is! The big 'P' causes so many changes, it's hard not to feel self-conscious about your bod or compare yourself with others. The important thing is not to get hung up about it. Instead, have fun with your appearance and get to know and love the person you are becoming – you and your body are going to be together for the long haul, so it makes sense to become the best of friends, right?

me and the
glam girl squad

What's the hurry?

I want ladybumps, I want to be kissed, I want to wear a bra... **I WANT IT NOW.**

I have ladybumps. Sadie has none. This makes her sad. I want to be allowed out later than 8pm like Bella, and Angel wants to wear movie star-esque make-up to school.

We're all in such a rush to do or get the things we think will make our lives substantially better, that we sometimes forget to enjoy just being a girl in the world.

That's the effect of puberty y'know.

One day you think you want to be grown up, the next you want to revert back to playing with dolls, although according to Bella, you'll still feel like this at 17! In fact, she thinks it's totally cool to play with Barbie. She has an entire collection and super-styles their do's by cutting mohawks and giving them purple streaks!

But, if the thought of periods scares you, yet you want to wear a bra, you're not alone, chica.

At Angel's super-swanky boarding school, some of the older girls persuaded her to bunk school and hang out with the boys from the equally swanksville boys' school across town. Angel thought it might be cool.

She was wrong, wrong, wrong.

"...SO, I HEAD INTO TOWN TO HANG WITH SOME MAJOR LEAGUE CUTIES, RIGHT? AND YEP, THAT'S EXACTLY WHAT THEY WERE.

ESPECIALLY AARON. HE WAS CUTENESS WITH A SUPER-SIZED CHERRY ON THE TOP. HE TOLD ME I LOOKED HOT. I ACCEPTED HIS COMPLIMENT WITH A SMILE. THEN HE TRIED TO KISS ME. 'WOAH, DUDE, NOT SO FAST' I HOLLERED.

WHO DID HE THINK HE WAS? FOR SURE, I THOUGHT HE WAS CUTE, BUT I'VE ONLY EVER KISSED ONE BOY AND I WILL NOT KISS ANOTHER UNTIL I DECIDE.

Y'SEE, THAT'S THE THING ABOUT THIS PUBERTY LARK, JUST BECAUSE I HAVE BOSOMS AND A CURVY BEE-HIND DOESN'T MEAN I'M READY FOR ALL THINGS SMOOCHY SMOOCHES. YET I DO LIKE TO DIG ON BOYS, JUST FROM A DISTANCE.

I TOLD HIM POLITELY THAT I WAS NOT A GIRL THAT WOULD SIMPLY JUST KISS HIM, AND DO YOU KNOW WHAT? HE TOTALLY DUG ON THAT.

HE EVEN SENT ME A TEXT TELLING ME HOW MUCH RESPECT HE HAD FOR ME NOT HEADING TO SMOOCH-TOWN WITH HIM.

AS HE SHOULD, I AM A PINK-THINKIN' PINK LADY OF FABULOUSNESS AFTER ALL! ..."

The transition from girls' world to womansville is not easy, chica, so don't rush it. The urge to grow up quickly and do everything right now may seem mucho tempting, but don't miss out on being a girl in the world. Because let's face it, being a girl rocks.

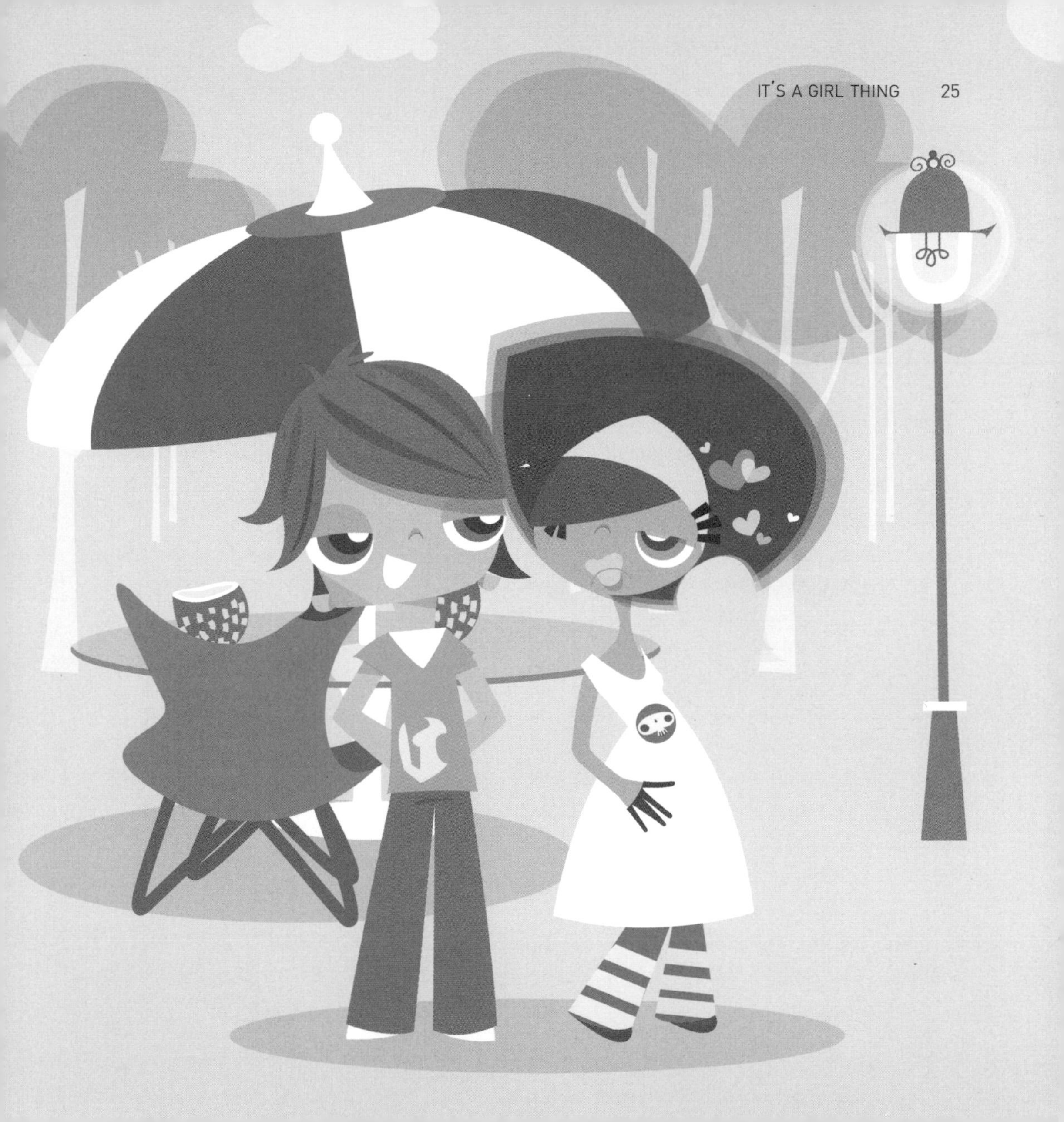

Why being a girl rocks...

There are a million zillion reasons why being a girl rocks.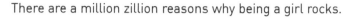

An ability to accessorise, being able to watch Audrey, Marilyn and Jane Mansfield movies back to back and wearing pink on a daily basis are just a few of my personal favourites, but what about you? What makes you feel jump-in-the-air happy that you're a girl?

Start by making a list here, then copy it on to your pinboard, into your journal, or get your art-girl on and create a collage with pictures and words and just keep adding to it – that way, you'll have a permanent reminder of why being a girl in the world is total fabulousity on a girl-shaped stick!

Why do you think being a girl rocks?

....
....
....
....
....
....
....
....
....
....
....
....

re-inacting our
fave film

Celebrate Girlsville

To be a girl is to be fabulous. Fact.

That's why the Pink Ladies and I have created our very own 'Celebrate Girlsville' list – a list of all the things a girl must do to officially celebrate Girlsville!

Tick what you've already done on our list, then do the rest. NOW!

Have you ever...

Cut your own fringe?

Tried an extreme sport? ✓

Invented code names for your crushes so that you could gossip undetected? ✓

Eaten a whole tub of Ben & Jerry's ice cream? ✓

Had a DVD-a-thon with your BFF? ✓

Written a list of all the things to do by the time you're 20? ✓

Had a dramatic change of hairstyle? ✓

Written a love letter? ✓

Customised your clothes until there were sequins on everything? ✓

Sent it? ✓

Sung in public? ✓

Made it to the front of the mosh pit at a gig? ✓

Made your own jewellery? ✓

Camped out overnight? ✓

Eaten sushi? ✓

Add your own 'Celebrate Girlsville' tasks right here:

....
....
....
....
....
....
....
....
....
....
....
....
....
....
....
....
....

....
....
....
....
....
....
....
....
....
....
....
....
....
....
....
....

Being a girl

...when it comes to body type, there's no right or wrong.

So, despite all the crazy, hazy things that happen during the big 'P' makeover, being a girl is pretty awesome, right?

So why is it that even the most pink-thinkin' of girls still look in the mirror and compare their sweet selves to celeb-types thinking that's the way they're supposed to look?

Girls, you are wrong, wrong, wrong.

Yep, the big 'P' brings some serious body changes and can make you feel allsorts of unsure of yourself as your straight-up-and-down beauty*licious bod begins to become curvier and more womanly. The trick is not to let it, because when it comes to body type, there's no right or wrong. Every pink-thinkin' chica knows that the most important beauty*licious body type is a healthy type!

Hair – why is it there?

I love my pink tresses of fabulousity. Fact.

What I don't love however, is the arrival of all this crazy amount of extra hair that has sprouted all over my bod.

I was freaked.

At first it was all soft, but as it's grown, it has become thicker and coarse which is major-league embarrassmondo when you're getting changed in front of your gal-pals in the dressing room.

I was freaked x100 because seeing hair growing not only on your legs, but under your arms and between your legs and even on my top lip, is slightly freaky.

Still, I may not like the way it looks, but I do know that it serves a purpose. No, it does, honest! It's Mumma Nature's way of adding protection to our delicate sensitive areas – which, in the grand scheme of things is pretty damn cool really.

So, can I get rid of this extra hair?
The goods news is, while it is there for your protection, it doesn't have to stay. Some people get rid of the hair under their arms so that it doesn't show when they're wearing their cute-as-a-button vests or sweetsville summer dresses, and some people remove the hair on their legs when it starts to become really noticeable, but a word of warning, it's best not to remove the hair between your legs because this can aggravate the sensitive skin down there.

Fuzz free – the facts

Now, you may not pay any attention to your hair growth, you might decide you wanna be rid of it right away or you might just want to wait a while and decide - to remove or not to remove - it's a pretty personal decision and it's completely up to you!

If you do want to be fuzz free, there are a whole lot of ways to whisk away unwanted hair...

Shaving
Shaving removes hair at skin level using a razor. These days, you can find razors that are disposable and designed especially for girls. These make it easier than ever to reach places with dips and curves, like the underarm area.

* ✫ **Why shaving rocks.** It's cheap, quick and painless.
* ✫ **Why shaving sucks.** Hair returns very quickly because it grows very quickly, usually within a couple of days.

Waxing
Waxing uses warm wax to remove hair. Because waxing has a major-league 'ouch' factor – you've got to pull the wax from your skin really quickly, much like you would a plaster – it's not the most painless method, but you do get a super-smooth, long lasting result.

* ✫ **Why waxing rocks.** Waxing has the best long-term effects, because it pulls hair out right from the root. After waxing, hair grows back in approximately three to four weeks.
* ✫ **Why waxing sucks.** 'Ouch!' Need I say more? Also you have to let the hair grow out quite a bit before you can wax again, which means having to put up with that in-between troublesome stubble.

Mittens

Mittens work like sandpaper, they're made of an abrasive material and you wear the mitten on your hand and rub the skin surface to remove hair.

* **Why mittens rock.** They're inexpensive and you don't have to worry about nicks or cuts.
* **Why mittens suck.** If you rub too hard you'll hurt yourself.

Depilatories

Apart from being a ridiculously silly word that I can't pronounce, depilatories are foams, gels, lotions and creams that dissolve the hair chemically below the skin's surface. You apply the cream, wait for 5-7 minutes, and then wipe the cream and dissolved hair away.

* **Why depilatories rock.** They're totally painless ways to remove hair and the hair stays away longer than it does if you shave.
* **Why depilatories suck.** They can smell a little bit – actually quite a bit!

Epilating

These hand-held systems look like an electric shaver and are generally battery operated. They have pinching mechanisms that work like teeny-tiny tweezers to pull the hairs from the root.

* **Why epilating rocks.** They remove hair from the root so it takes much longer for the hair to grow back – epilating should leave you hairless for up to 5 weeks.
* **Why epilating sucks.** It hurts.
   A lot.
   And an epilator can be quite costly.

Skin deep

Spots, blemishes, pimples... no matter what you call them, zits are the pits. Nearly eight out of ten girls will have some form of breakout and you can blame this (and lots of other stuff!) on those pesky hormones again. Even though your skin needs a certain amount of oil to keep it supple, during the big 'P' makeover, it sometimes produces more than it actually needs. This can cause your pores to get blocked and create real life, boo-worthy spots.

Pink Lady, Bella, knows a lot about spots; her pimples made her a super shy girl (which is mucho hard to believe right now!) but she beat the blushes and now digs who she is with and without spots, which officially makes her the Bod Squad's zit-bustin' queen!

"...IT'S TRUE, ZITS REALLY ARE THE PITS. I USED TO SUFFER REALLY BAD ACNE ON MY FACE AND ON MY BACK AND IT MADE ME FEEL SO TOTALLY, TOTALLY ICKSVILLE-BLAH, I COULDN'T EVEN LEAVE THE HOUSE.

THE REASON FOR THIS KILLER TWO-YEAR BREAK-OUT WAS DOWN TO THE OVERACTIVE OIL-PRODUCING GLANDS THAT TEND TO BE CONCENTRATED IN WHAT IS KNOWN AS THE T-ZONE, WHICH RUNS ACROSS THE FOREHEAD AND DOWN THE NOSE AND CHIN — WHICH IS PRIME ZIT TERRITORY. THERE ARE ALSO A LOT OF OIL GLANDS IN THE CHEST AND BACK, WHICH IS WHY I WAS A WALKING, TALKING SPOT.

EXCEPT I WASN'T.

I DID HAVE BAD ACNE, AND IT DID FEEL LIKE THOSE PESKY PIMPLES WERE PICKING ON ME, BUT ALMOST EVERYONE WILL HAVE A BATTLE WITH BLEMISHES AT SOME POINT AND IT'S IMPORTANT TO DIG ON YOURSELF WITH OR WITHOUT SPOTS..."

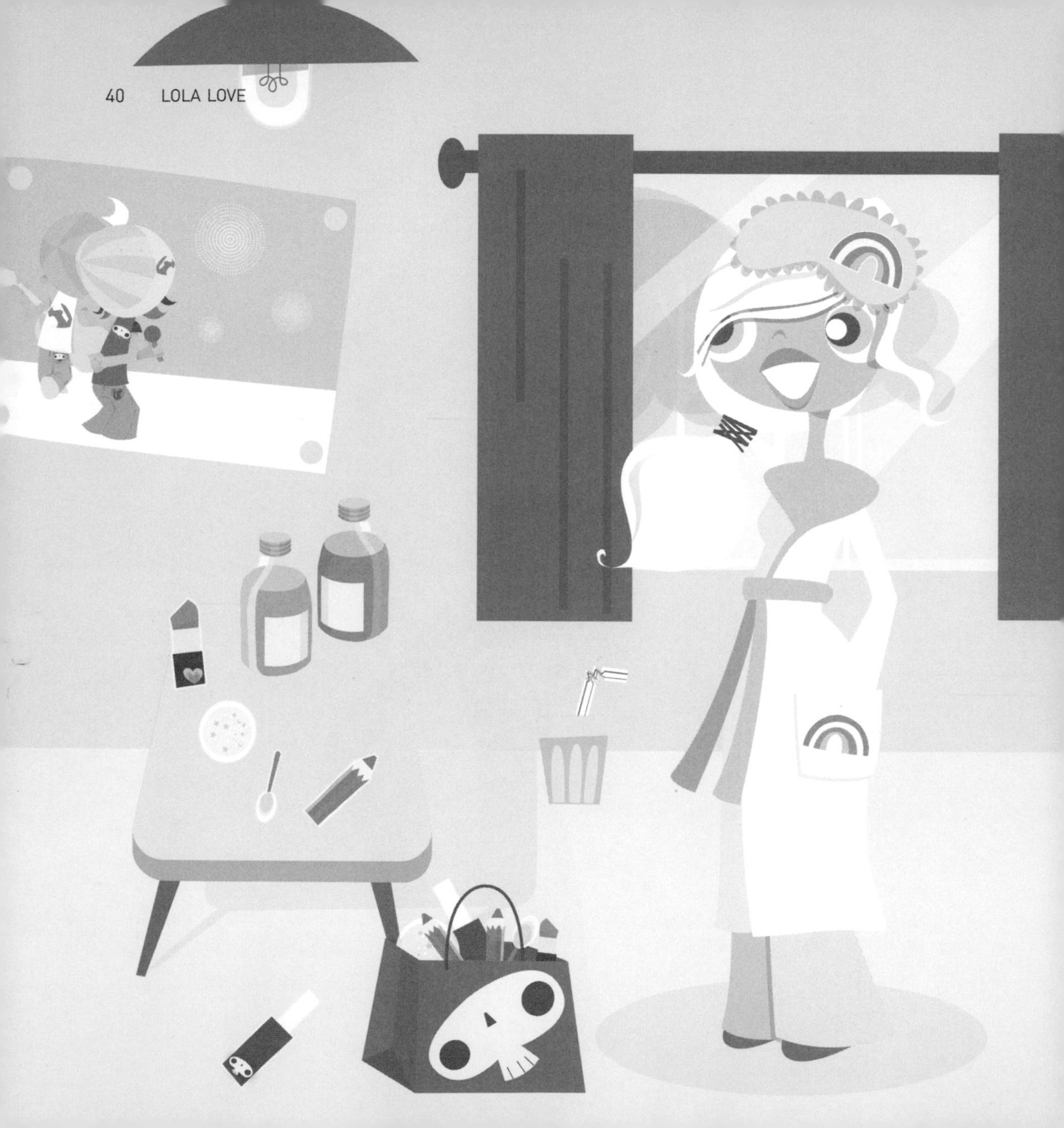

Spot check

If you want to maximise your chances of clear skin, memorise these five bod squad skin-happy points right now.

✮ Establish a twice-daily routine of cleansing, toning and moisturising – it really is a girl's best friend! Determining your skin type can help you decide what skin care prods will work for you – here's how to figure out what skin you're in:

Oily – skin has a noticeable sheen. If you blot with a tissue, you will probably see oil on the tissue.

Combination – has an oily t-zone – the area on the forehead, nose and chin.

Dry – skin has dry, flaky areas but can still be prone to breakouts.

Sensitive – skin has a tendency to react to various chemicals and fragrances in skin products.

Use specialist face-washes or cleansers – different kinds of skin require different kinds of care. What works to get rid of spots on your gal-pal will not necessarily banish your blemishes, so check out the skin care aisle at your chemist, read the labels carefully and find one that's right for your skin type.

Tip: Products that contain benzoyl peroxide are great because they help to reduce oil and get rid of dead skin but WARNING! Benzoyl peroxide can irritate sensitive skin. Before putting it on your face, test a little on the inside of your wrist to see if it gives you a rash. If it does, then chica, don't use it!

☆ Look after your general health and wellbeing – what we put in our beauty*licious bods deffo affects our skin condition, so be sure to drink lots of water, which will clean out the icky toxins and re-hydrate your skin – it's the ultimate beautifier!

☆ Don't squeeze, pick or pop your spots – even if there is a neon sign flashing 'squeeze me, pick me, pop me!' As tempting as it might be, it'll only make them worse.

☆ Be patient – spots don't disappear overnight.

If pimples are making you feel like a resident of sucksville, talk to your doctor. Severe out-of-control acne calls for medical attention. Your doctor can prescribe special creams or pills that are stronger than products available without a prescription.

Ask the bod squad!

I've got a big spot on my nose. How can I get rid of it?
Your fingertips are home to more pimple-producing oils than you could ever imagine. So no matter how tempting it might be to pop the mini-volcano that's threatening to erupt on your nose – DON'T. This can make it worse and cause it to flare up or scar the skin. Instead, keep the area clean and allow it to disappear in its own time.

What can I do to help prevent spots?
Make sure you wash your face every day, eat lots of fruit and vegetables and drink lots of toxin-flushing water. It's a myth that chocolate and greasy food cause spots, but eating well will definitely make your skin healthier and less prone to pimples. Spots really do effect most teens, even li'l miss perfecto Eva Satine has been known to have a pimple once in a while, but if you're really bothered about them, speak to your parents and ask them to help you arrange a trip to the docs to get 'em checked out.

Is there anything I can use on my spots that doesn't have harsh chemicals in it?
There is! There are lots of alternative or natural remedies for skin problems out there. Different things work for different people. Many people put masks on their faces (made of clay, fruits, vegetables, mayonnaise, oatmeal, seaweed and other natural stuff – do an internet search for natural spot remedies – you'll get a whole host of possibilities to choose from). Other popular natural skin remedies include: steaming your face (holding it over a bowl of boiling water with a towel over your head) to open and unclog pores: or applying vitamin E to reduce the effect of scarring.

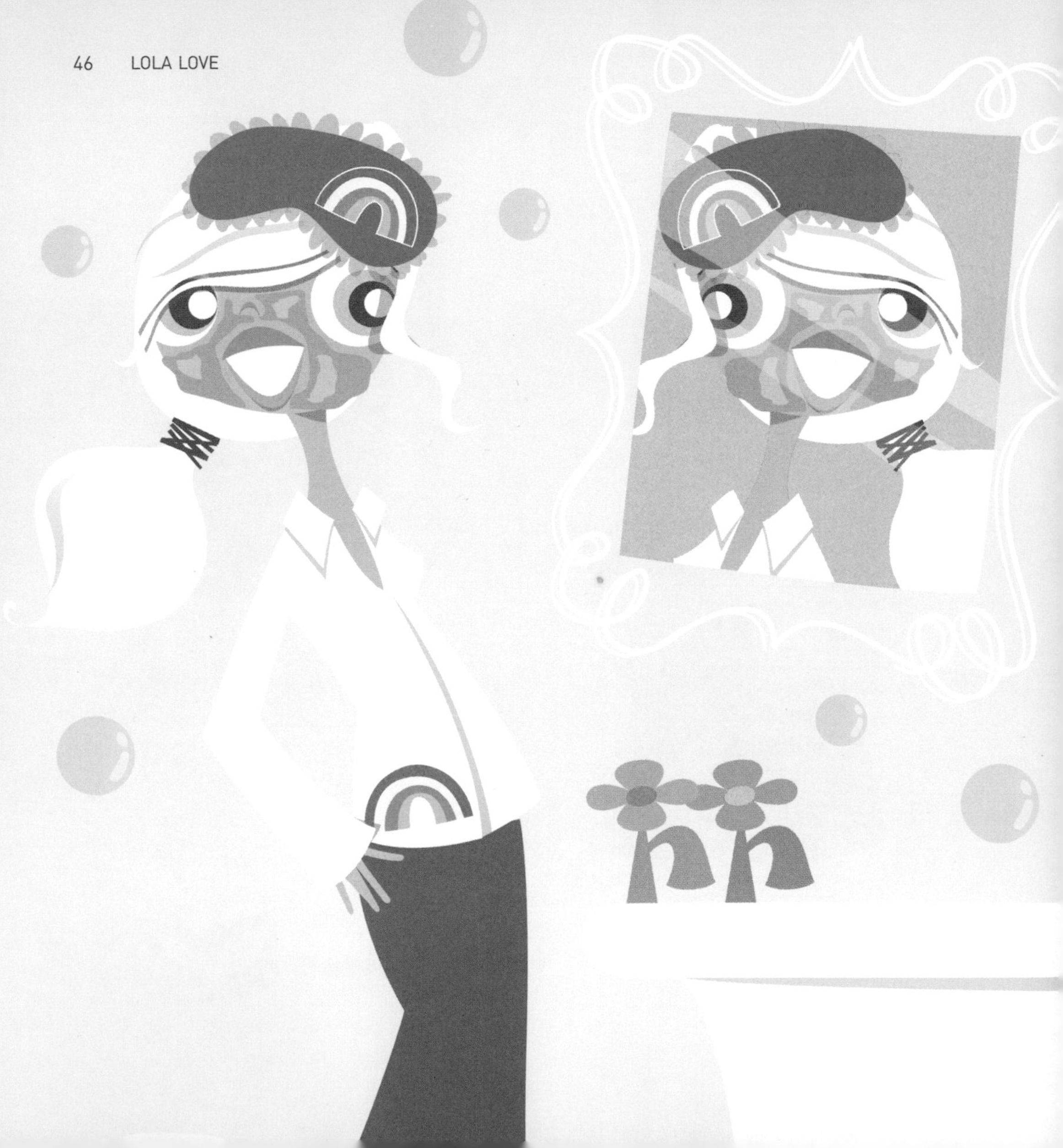

Try this: Bella's Banana Blemish Buster

This soothing DIY face-mask is great for pimple-prone skin and also tastes rather yummy too – except you really shouldn't eat it after it's been on your face, 'coz really gorgeous girl, that's just ick!

INGREDIENTS:

☆ 1 banana, preferably ripe (you can keep ripe bananas in the freezer. Let it thaw before using)
☆ 1 tbsp honey
☆ An orange or a lemon

PREPARATION:

☆ Mix the banana and honey together.
☆ Add a few drops of juice from an orange or a lemon.
☆ Apply to face for 15 minutes before rinsing with a cool washcloth.

Stress = an unhappy YOU

Okay, take a deep yoga-style breath, and let all your worries roll over that nervy yet so-very-pretty head of yours.

If you find that you're a messy, stressy type, then for the sake of your bod and your face – 'coz stressing can cause your skin to breakout too y'know – chill your boots.

If you don't give yourself that much-needed alone time that's all about you, every single day, your stress levels will sky rocket.

Not good.

What is good, however, is for you to have some 'all about you' time.

Time to think about all the things that happened throughout the day, time to plan pink domination, and time to spend doing the things you love to do.

Whether it's putting curls in your poker-straight hair, reading a book, writing in a journal or listening to your *tune du jour* on repeat, find something that puts you in your very own YOU zone.

My favourite end of week wind-down is to take a steamy bubble bath, put on my sweet-smelling pink PJ's, play my 'The Best of Doris Day' CD and curl up and read. Whether you're reading Jane Austen or Now magazine, all that matters is that you give yourself that much needed 'all-about-you' time.

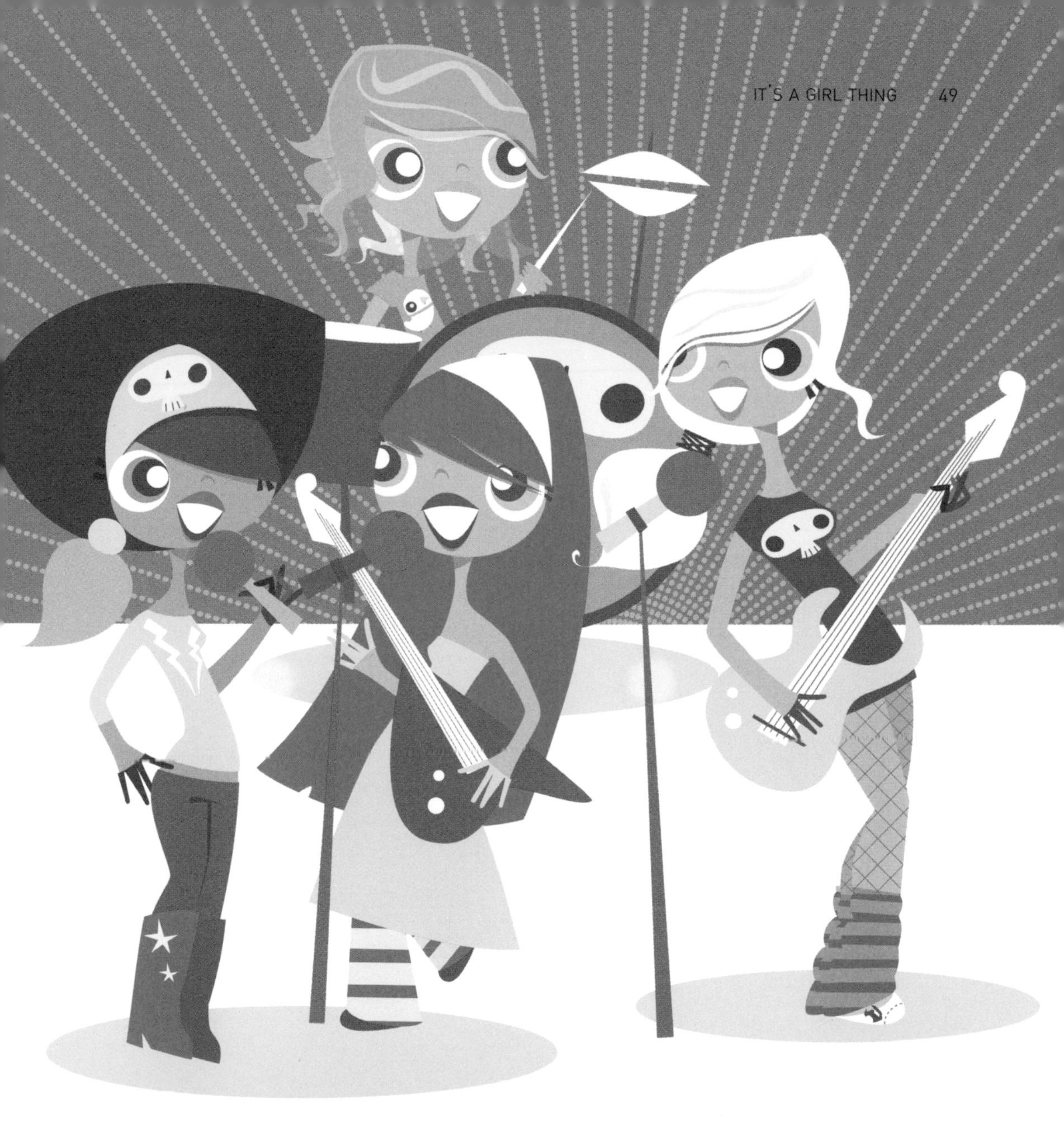

What are your favourite 'all-about-you' time de-stressers?

....

....

....

....

....

....

....

....

....

....

....

....

....

....

....

....

....

....

....

....

....

....

....

....

....

....

having a relaxing walk
with Sadie

Smile – you're bee–yoou–tiful!

As you know, a smile is the perfect accessory for any pink thinkin' laydee, but if, like our total inspiro-girl Ugly Betty – who is not even ugly, not one little bit – you have to wear a brace, the idea of flashing your gnashers in public can be pretty daunting, right?

It doesn't have to be. Braces are total Pink Lady smile enhancers and, if like a lot of people, your teeth aren't straight or maybe your upper and lower jaws aren't the same size, your dentist might recommend that you go see an orthodontist. They are the kings and queens of all things brace-like and will decide whether you need to wear braces or not, coz they're clever like that.

Get ready chica, here comes the science bit: Braces, or smile enhancers as we like to call them, straighten teeth by putting steady pressure on them and by staying in place for a certain amount of time. Most people just need regular braces with wires and rubber bands - the wires on the braces help to move the teeth, and the rubber bands help to correct the way the teeth line up – cool, huh?

Braces are total Pink Lady smile enhancers...

If your teeth need a little extra help, you may have to wear head or neck gear with wires attached to your teeth – just like our super sweet, fave TV girl, Betty Suarez. If you do, don't panic! You probably will only have to wear it at night or when you're at home in the evening – and just think, it'll be working to create you the most killer watt, dazzling smile – don't be fearful, instead, work it like it's Prada, sweetie!

Everyone has to wear their smile enhancers for different lengths of time, but most people usually wear them for about two years. When your new, enhanced, sweet-as-sugar smile is unleashed, you may need to wear a retainer, which is a small, hard piece of plastic with metal wires or a thin piece of plastic shaped like a mouth guard. Retainers make sure your teeth don't go wandering back to their original places. Your retainer will be specially moulded to fit your newly straightened teeth.

Life with a smile enhancer – the facts

Smile enhancers act like magnets for food, so you need to keep your teeth especially clean while you have them on. You'll want to brush after meals and be extra careful to get out any food that gets stuck in your braces.

Avoid foods that are a problem for smile enhancers - stay away from popcorn, hard and sticky candy, and especially gum. Sugary sodas and juices can cause a problem too, because the sugar stays on your teeth and may cause tooth decay. You can have these drinks, but be sure to brush afterwards.

Because braces put pressure on your teeth, you might feel uncomfortable once in a while, especially after the orthodontist makes adjustments. If you have pain, ask your parentals if you can have a pain reliever.

If you ever have a loose wire or bracket, or a wire that is poking you, you should see the orthodontist right away to get it taken care of – don't suffer!

If you're wearing a smile enhancer, don't be afraid to flash it – it will make a shout-out-loud statement to the world that you totally dig on your sweet self. For sure, they can be inconvenient, but they're definitely worth the trouble. When will you know for sure? On the day your braces are removed and you can see your new, super-enhanced smile, of course!

Don't sweat it!

The big '**P**' can stink.
Literally.

Along with all the extra oil your body is producing, your sweat glands are working overtime too. This is called perspiration, and when the sweat comes into contact with the air, it dries and goes stale, which means you can end up with a rather unpleasant not-so-sweet smelling odour that we know as BO (body odour).

Ick.

What can I do to stop my armpits sweating?
There's nothing you can do about sweat.

Rude.

It's your bod's way of regulating your temperature and ensuring that you stay cool.
However, you can do something about that pesky BO – whoop, whoop!

BO Bashing

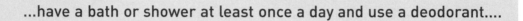

...have a bath or shower at least once a day and use a deodorant....

Your weapons of choice in the battle of BO are:
Deodorants – contain chemicals that mask odours.
Antiperspirants – contain chemicals that slow down or block the production of sweat.

Deodorants and antiperspirants are applied under your arms, usually in the morning after you shower. Some girls re-apply after PE or simply when they want to feel fresh again, which is more than cool, just be sure to apply them to clean skin. It doesn't do any good to re-apply after you've perspired, in fact, it can be a whole lot worse.
There are many types of deodorant and antiperspirant products available in chemists and supermarkets and they come in lots of different forms:

☆ Roll-on   ☆ Solid stick   ☆ Gel   ☆ Spray

There are some great natural brands on the market that don't contain any chemicals but still do the job. Try a few different forms and brands so you can decide which one works best for you. To maintain a maximo sweet-smellin' you, have a bath or shower at least once a day and use a deodorant to keep fresh.

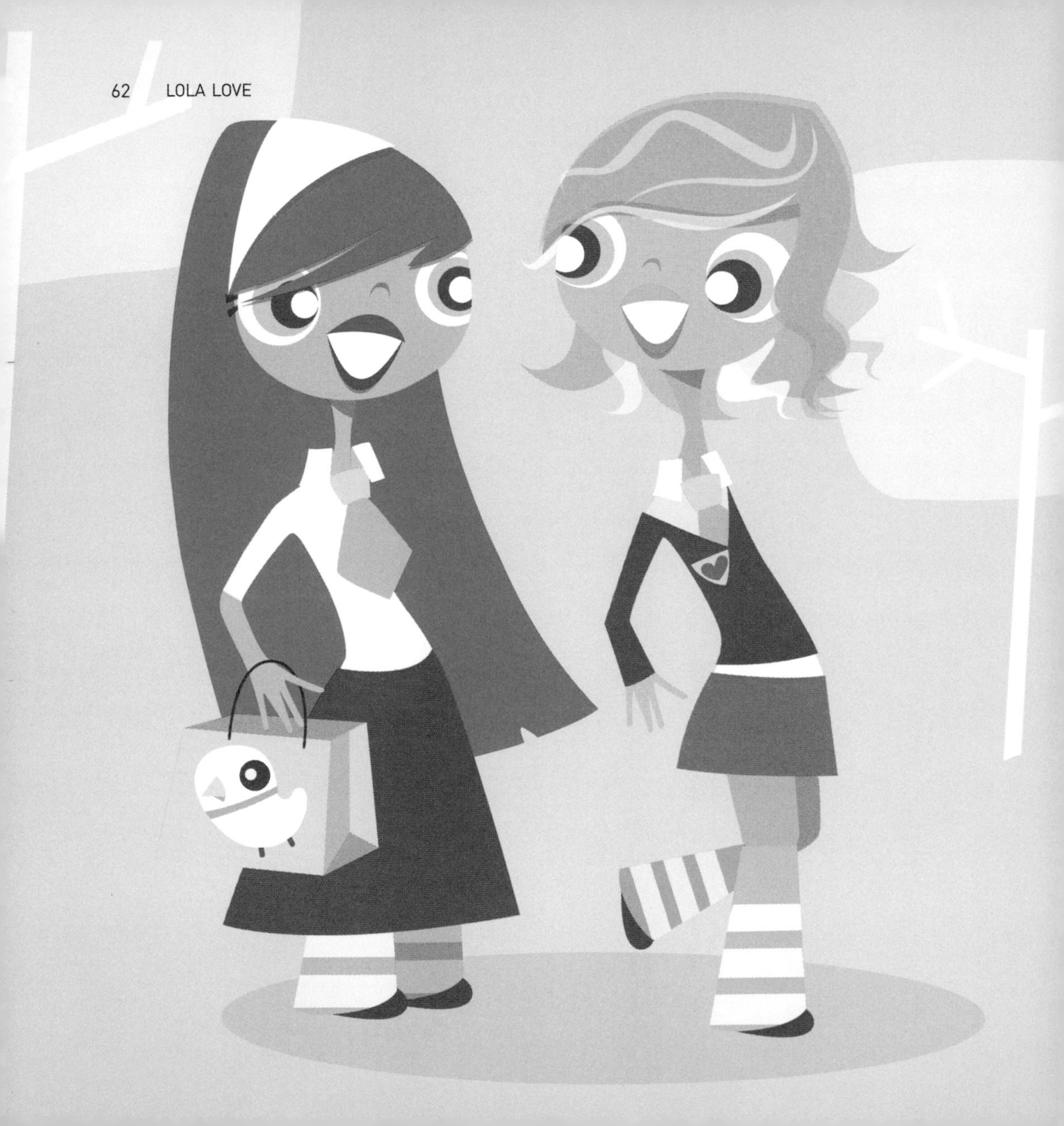

What's normal down there?

The bod squad go below the waist and talk vaginas.
Yep.
Vaginas.

It's not a dirty word y'know, although it does make Sadie and I giggle behind our hands like Geisha girls when we say it. But that's because nobody actually says it. Yet it's crucial to become familiar with what's up down there as you grow and change – which is why, right now, we're talking vaginas.

"I'm paranoid my vagina looks weird? What is this area meant to look like?"
Every girl looks different and, just like boobs and bums, there is no such thing as a 'normal' vagina. Phew!

The area you can see most easily when you look in the mirror is called the vulva and it's made up of two pairs of lips. These lips are called labia and they can vary in size and length and aren't necessarily symmetrical. The colour can vary as well, ranging from light pink to cocoa brown, so don't stress if you think the flesh on your vulva is an odd shade – it's perfectly fine!

Once you hit puberty, you will start growing hair around your vulva. Some girls have lots of thick pubic hair down there, while others just have a light covering. And not everyone has black pubic hair, so if yours is a lighter shade than your friend's, no stress!

Sometimes I think my vagina smells. Can other people smell it through my clothes?
As icky as it sounds, every girl's vagina has a faint smell most of the time. You're probably more sensitive to the odour because you're focussed on your own body. But don't worry, it's unlikely anyone else can smell it. However, if the smell ever becomes stronger, you should go see your doctor for a health check because it could be bacterial vaginosis, an infection that can be easily treated with antibiotics. Never be too scared or too embarrassed to go see your doctor at any point through the big 'P' makeover. They'll happily put your mind at ease about any of your concerns or worries.

Periods

Ick.

That was my first word when I discovered my period had started. Shortly after that, I fainted.

Y'see, I saw blood and didn't know what it was or where it was from. That's because I didn't actually know what a period was. My mum never talked about girl stuff with me. Nothing, not a thing, nada. Some parents are just like that.

But getting your period and not knowing anything about it is big-time scary.

Luckily, Angel's mum, a bigger, slightly rounder version of Angel, is totally the opposite to my mum and is all about the talking. She gave me a sanitary towel, which was like some crazy-shaped nappy for my knickers, and explained everything...

"...GETTING YOUR PERIOD MEANS YOUR BODY HAS REACHED THE STAGE WHERE IT'S ABLE TO HAVE A BABY, NOT THAT YOU'RE GOING TO OBVIOUSLY, BUT ONCE A MONTH, IT GETS REVVED-UP FOR POSSIBLE MOTHERHOOD. WHEN YOUR PERIOD STARTS, YOUR OVARIES RELEASE AN EGG THAT TRAVELS THROUGH YOUR FALLOPIAN TUBES INTO YOUR UTERUS. IF THE EGG ISN'T FERTILISED BY A SPERM, IT WILL BREAK UP – ALONG WITH THE WOMB LINING – AND LEAVE YOUR BODY. THAT'S YOUR PERIOD!..."

From then on, I've been like one of those Boy Scout dudes, prepared.

Periods can come and go and can be irregular at first, so it's a good idea to have a towel or a tampon with you just in case one starts - I carry an individually wrapped towel in my pink, polka-dot bag - they're perfect for saving you from potentially embarrassment-o sitches!

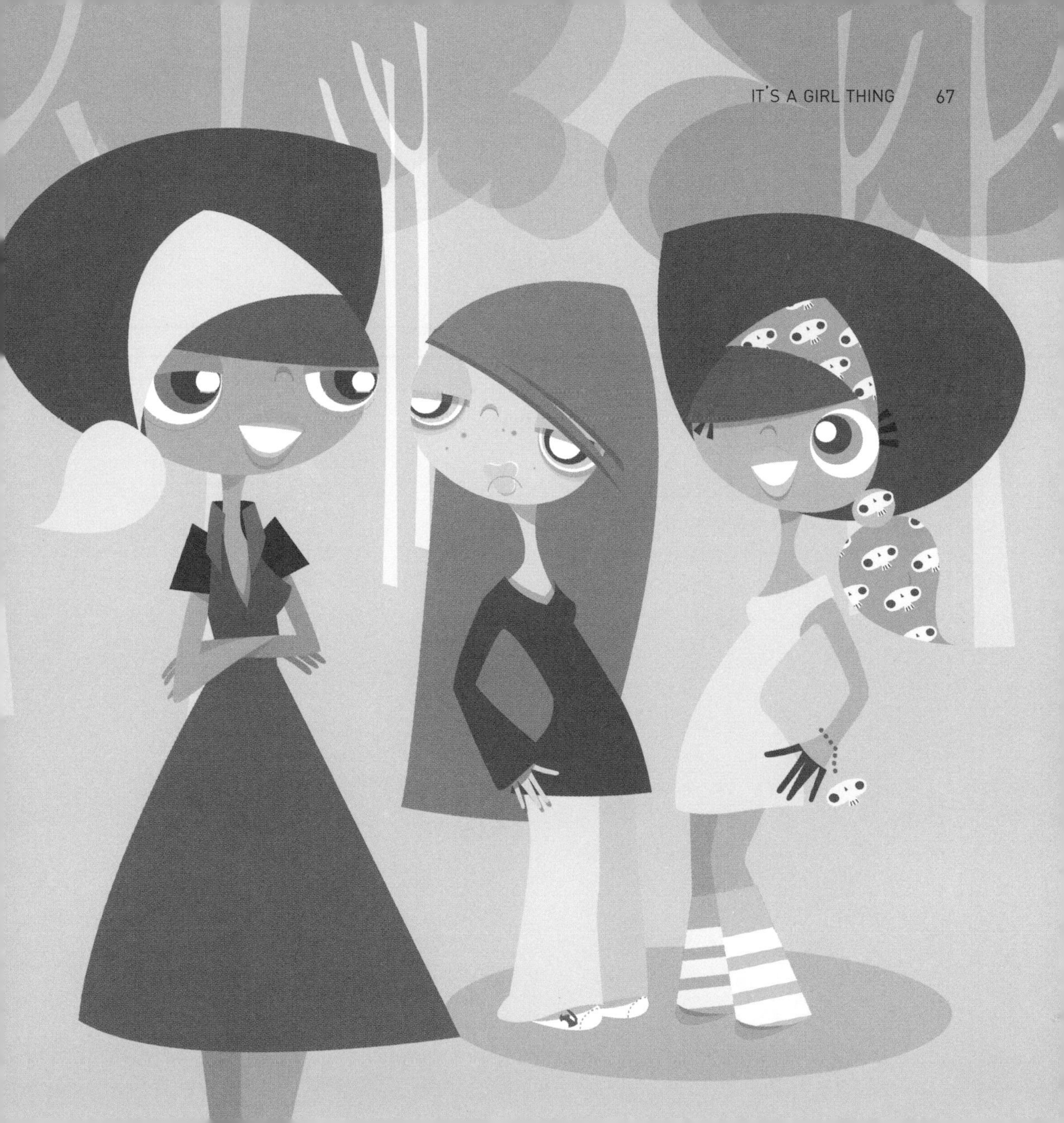

Take a dip!

Now, it's not like us Pink Ladies **EVER** need an excuse to pamper our sweet selves, but when the crimson wave comes riding into town, it can cause cramp-like pains and make you feel slightly icky-blah, so a long soak in a full-to-the-brim bath is by far the nicest thing you can do for yourself.

Don't worry, the blood doesn't flow as fast while you're in the water, keeping clean during period time is mucho important AND the warm water will ease any uncomfy cramps you might be feeling.

Ahhhhhhhh.

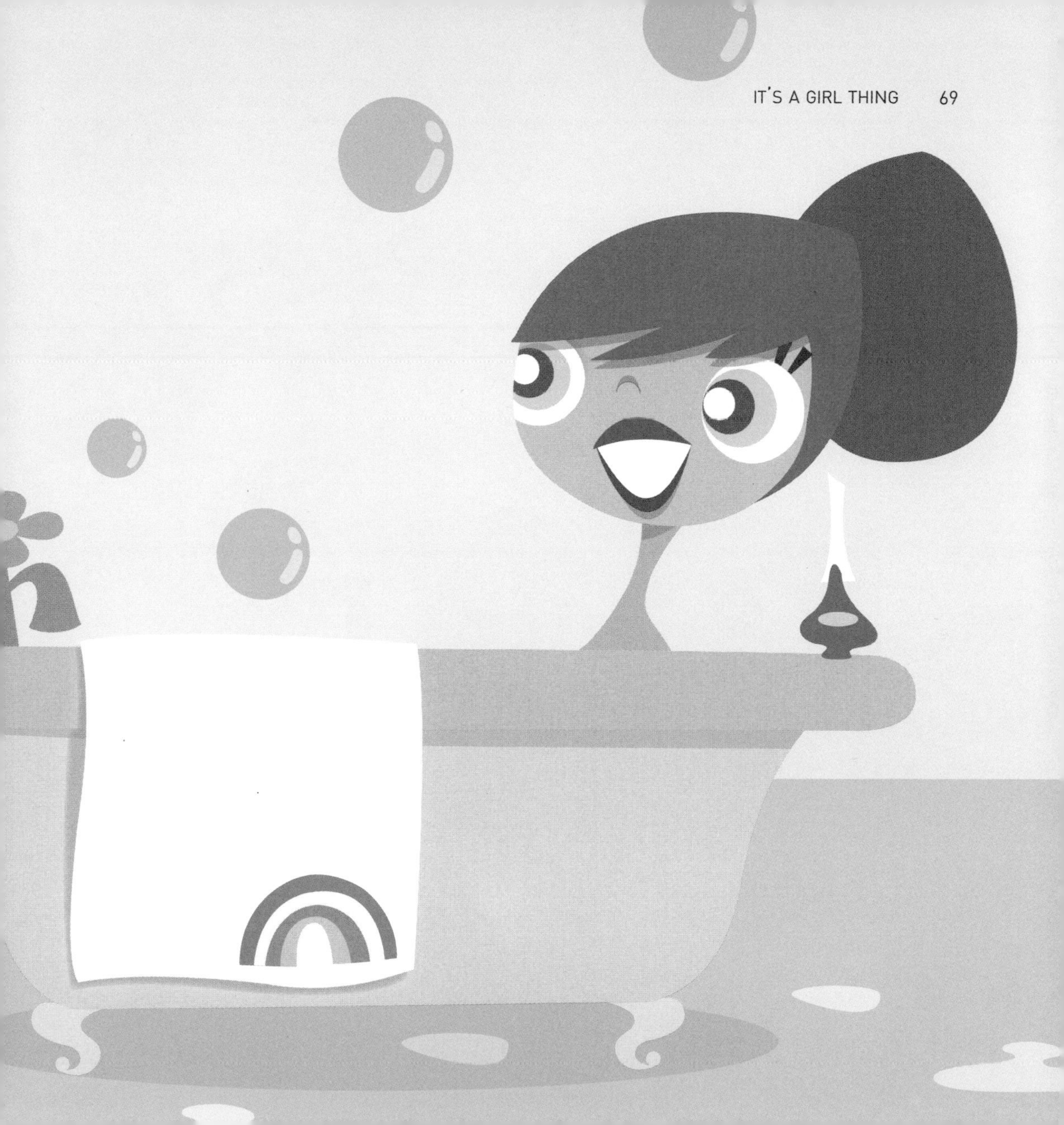

The Bod Squad's yummy honey ice-cream bubble bath recipe

Banish the blahs by relaxing in a soothing bubble bath overflowing with ice-cream flavoured yummy honey bubbles that you've made yourself! Honey is nature's silky moisturiser and guaranteed to sweeten your mood!

Ingredients:
* ☆ 1 cup light olive oil
* ☆ 1/2 cup honey
* ☆ 1/2 cup unscented liquid soap
* ☆ 1 tablespoon vanilla extract

Directions:
* ☆ Measure the oil into a medium bowl, then carefully stir in remaining ingredients until mixture is fully blended.
* ☆ Pour into a clean plastic bottle with a tight-fitting stopper or lid.
* ☆ Shake gently before using and you'll have enough for four large luxurious bubble filled baths.
* ☆ Swirl desired amount into the bathtub under running water - then step in - bliss.

Your period cycle. The It's A Girl Thing circle of your cycle!

an example of your 28 day cycle in a lovely pie chart

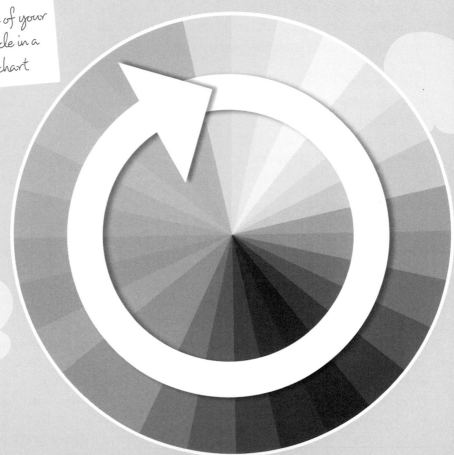

Day one

Your Emo – You might feel super tired, but PMS symptoms will lessen – yay!

Your Looks – Any PMS spots you have begin to clear up

Your Bod – the lining of the uterus leaves your body in the form of a period

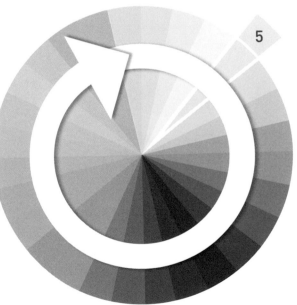

Day 5

Your Emo – smile – you're feeling mucho happier!

Your Looks – your skin becomes clearer and less oily

Your Bod – your period has nearly finished – happy days!

Day 14
Your Emo – You feel full of fabulousness
Your Looks – you might have a slight tummy ache and get a gooey discharge
Your bod – Ovulation: egg is released.

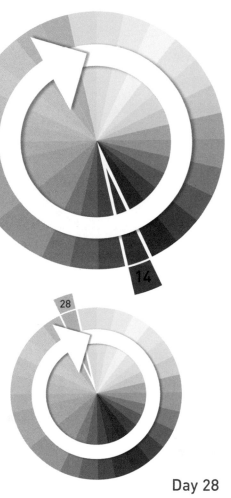

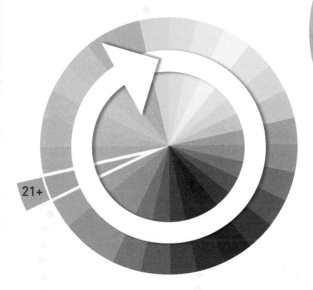

Day 21+
Your Emo – You're stressy, antsy and irritable
Your looks – you may be getting more spots than usual and your tummy might be bloated
Your bod – Your body is in hormone overdive

Day 28
Cycle begins again

day 14 and I feel fabulous!

Tame your period pain

There are certain parts of getting your period that take some getting used to. Like deciding which sanitary protection to use or inserting a tampon for the first time, but with a bit of practise both of these become a do-able part of the cycle. Then there's the other stuff.

The stuff that is slightly trickier to get your head round is, tripping unexpectedly in the street, yelling at your parentals, craving potato and gravy or bursting into tears over an episode of your favourite soap.

The bod squad's Bella explains everything...

1. **Tender boobs –** They may feel like you're being prodded with a red-hot poker during your period, so for days like these,make sure you have a comfy bra.

2. **Grumpy lumps –** When your hormones are raging, it's easy to snap at the people around you because your brain is lacking a chemical called seratonin – this can make you mucho irritable. To get the seratonin pumpin' get your exercise on, chica!

3. **Attack of the pimple –** Your skin is more prone to pimples during the first couple of days of your period – grr. Be sure to clean and exfoliate daily to remove dead skin cells.

4. **The cramps –** As the lining of your uterus breaks down, it can cause tummy cramping. For some it may be a dull ache but for others, cramp pains can have them doubled up in agony. To ease the pain, try a long soak in a warm bath – don't worry, your period flow slows down when in water or hold a hot water bottle on your tummy while watching your fave DVD.

5. **Mucho clumsy –** When your period arrives, it may feel like your sense of co-ordination ups and leaves.

Rude.

Yes, it's annoying, but it's totally normal in the few days leading up to your period starting. And yep, like most of the other symptoms you experience, it's caused by those pesky hormones racing through your body.

if I close my eyes
maybe they
will go away...

One of the best ways to tame your PMT symptoms is to recognise them in the first place! When Bella first started her period, we would all suffer the Rage. She would flip out so very completely at anything and everything we started to think she didn't like us anymore!

"IT'S TRUE, JUST BEFORE I GOT MY PERIOD, I WOULD TURN INTO A COMPLETE MONSTER. I'D FLY OFF THE HANDLE AT ANYONE, MY BUDS, MY COOLIO AGO-GO DAD, EVEN STRANGERS!

LUCKILY, I HAD THE PINK LADIES TO PICK UP ON MY ISSUES. THEY NOTICED THAT MY BLACK MOODS TOTALLY TIED IN TO THE TIMES I NEEDED TO BORROW TAMPONS (I'M REALLY UNDER PREPARED!). WHILE LOLA, ANGEL AND SADIE TRIED TO SOOTHE ME WITH QUIET MOVIE NIGHTS AND CHOCOLATE (IN HEALTHY-ISH QUANTITIES, MY SUPER COOL DAD WAS ALL ABOUT TEACHING ME SPECIAL YOGA POSITIONS THAT STRETCH THE RIGHT MUSCLES AND LOTS OF EVENING PRIMROSE OIL, A DIETRY SUPPLEMENT THAT CAN REALLY HELP CHILL OUT YOUR HORMONES.

THE BEST WAY TO FIGURE OUT WHAT'S HAPPENING TO YOU DURING YOUR PERIOD IS TO KEEP A DIARY AND MAKE A NOTE OF ANYTHING AND EVERYTHING YOU NOTICE, LIKE SPOTS ON A CERTAIN PART OF YOUR FACE (IF YOU GET LOADS ON YOUR CHIN, THEY'RE MOST LIKELY CAUSED BY THOSE PESKY HORMONES AT PERIOD TIME), GREASY HAIR, WEEPY OR ANGRY MOOD SWINGS, FOOD CRAVINGS – ANYTHING! ONCE YOU RECOGNISE THEM, YOU'LL BE READY FOR THEM!"

Got questions about that time of the month?
The Bod Squad are here to help!

Why haven't I started yet?
There's no set age for starting your period. They happen when your body's ready and your ovaries start working. Periods can start any time; the best way to predict when you'll start is to ask your female relatives when they started as it can be hereditary.

Don't stress: if they haven't happened yet, they're deffo in the post!

How long will my period last?
Periods tend to last between three and seven days and, although it may seem like you're losing a serious lot of blood, you're actually not. Your body only loses between 35 to 40ml of blood a month (about two tablespoons worth). Yes, you can say 'eeeeeeuuuwww!' now!

How can I lose the pain?
The dull ache of period pain can be as grim as extra maths homework, but you can make it better. A brisk walk will make your body's natural painkillers (endorphins) kick in. And while it might sound borin' snorin' it's true: drinking lots of water, eating well and getting to bed early all help. A lot. If you don't like taking painkillers, try soothing peppermint tea – mmmm.

Sanitary towels or tampons - what's best?
You should use whatever you feel comfy with, try both and see what works for you. Most girls start with towels (which line the inside of your knickers) because they're easy to use.

Towels come in a whole lot of different sizes so you can choose one to fit the shape of your body. They come in different thicknesses too, so you can choose one to suit the heaviness of your period. They have a sticky strip on the back that you press firmly to your pants to hold the towel in place – it's best to change your towel every few hours, even if your blood flow is not heavy. Don't flush your used towel down the loo, it can block pipes and is bad for the environment. Instead, wrap it up and throw them in the waste bin.

Tampons (which are inserted into your vagina) take a little bit of practice, but they come with instructions and if you read and follow them carefully, you'll find it easy to get the hang of them too. Tampons come in different sizes from mini to super plus, and the size you need depends on how heavy your period is, rather than on the size of your body. Once a tampon is in the right place in your vagina, you can't feel it at all, and you'll only need to change it every four hours. You can flush them down the toilet, but it's better for the environment if you dispose of them in the same way as towels.

How do I know when they're going to happen?
Your period may be very unpredictable for the first two years while you settle into your cycle, so if you're a bit up and down, while it might be totally inconvenient, please don't worry. Generally, you'll get a period every 26 to 28 days, but dramatic weight loss, stress, illness and big upheavals, like moving house or splitting up from a pesky boy can also muck up the frequency of your periods.

What's all this other stuff?
Don't fret. It's probably vaginal discharge, and it's perfectly normal – it's your body's way of keeping your vagina clean. But if it's smelly, discoloured or blood-stained and you get a burning sensation, check to see if you've left a tampon in. They should be changed every four to eight hours and removed at the end of a period.

Make your period day like any other by...

☆ Having fun with your Pink Ladies to take your mind off it
– organise a Film Friday and watch back-to-back Audrey
and Marilyn films – ahh, bliss!

☆ Eat chocolate and strawberries – they're so very deelish
and the perfect-o treat to self!

☆ Plugging yourself into a feel-good playlist and walking
round the block – any excuse to work those pink
legwarmers, right?

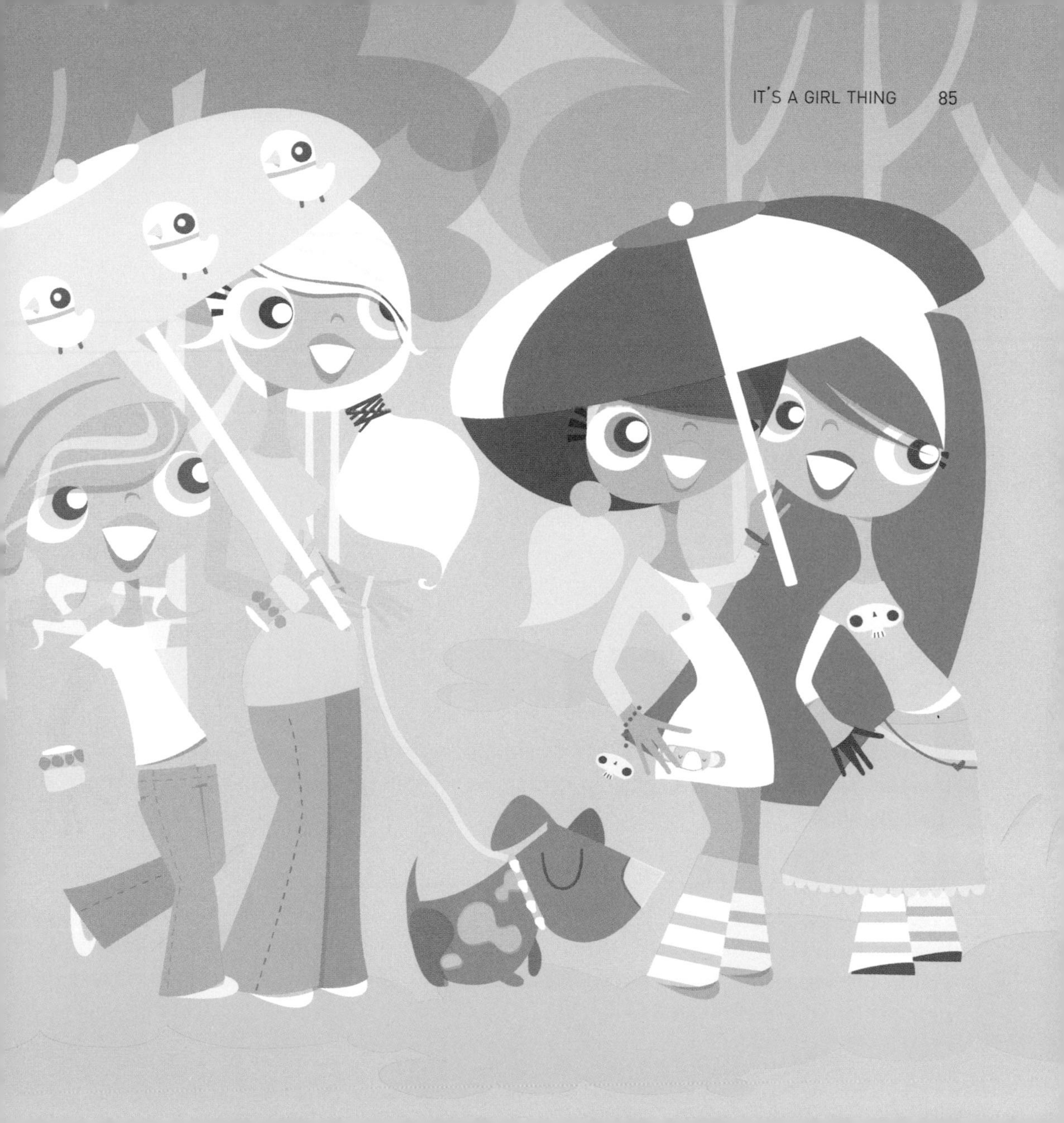

My lumps, my lovely Ladybumps!

Boobs, breasts, bangers, knockers, jugs, hooters, baps – whatever you call them, all girls get them eventually.

One minute there's nothing there, the next, there are boob-shaped ladybumps in your cute tight tee, what's going on?

I'll tell you what's going on, chica, yet another part of the big 'P' makeover! Boobs, breasts, bangers, knockers, jugs, hooters, baps – whatever you call them, all girls get them eventually.

Although trying to tell Pink Lady, Sadie, that is easier said than done.

She is still waiting for hers and gets mondo frustrated at their rude lack of growing ability. She measures them on a weekly basis and is constantly comparing her sweet petite self to the likes of evil Eva – grr.

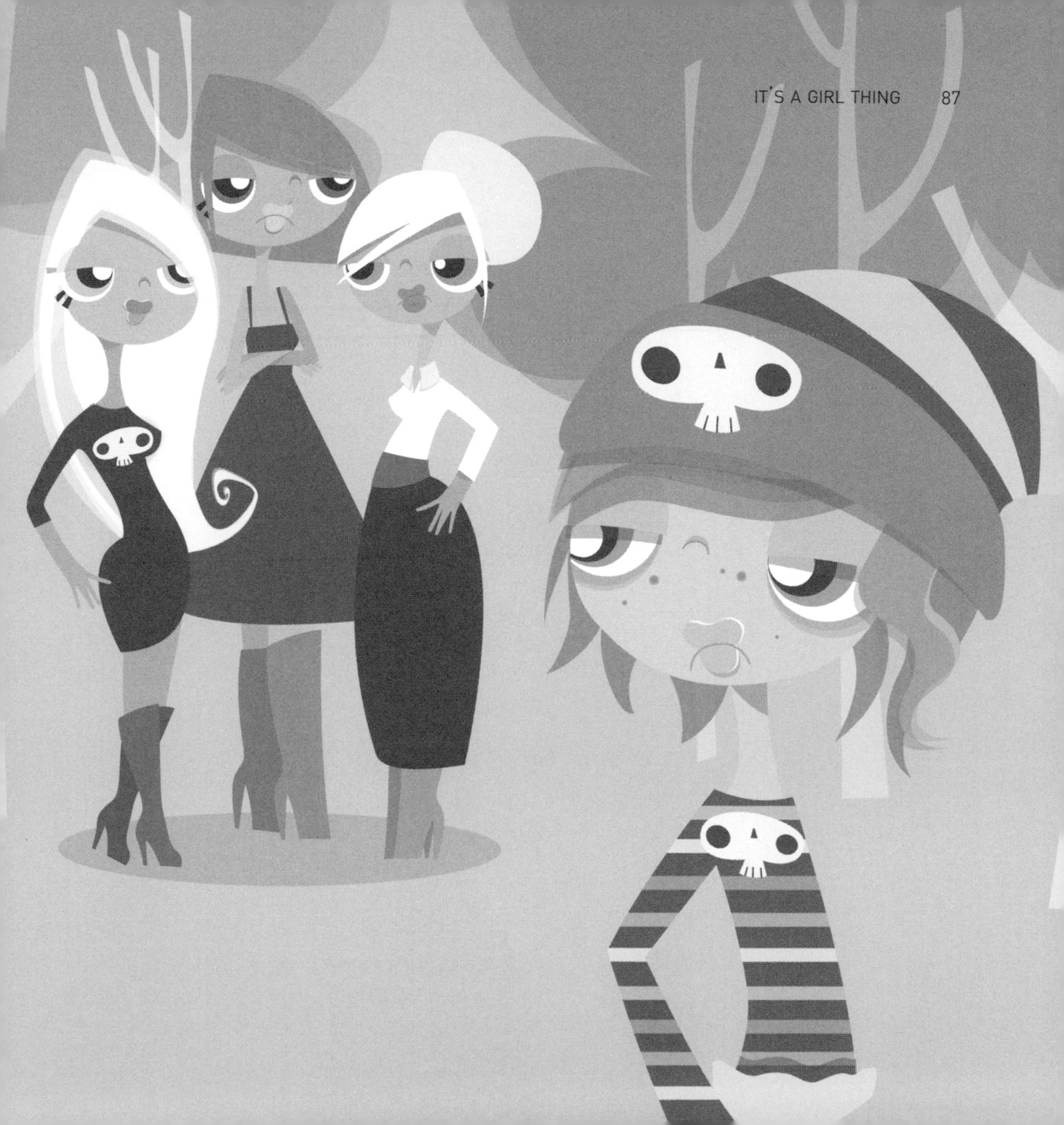

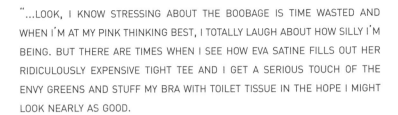

"...LOOK, I KNOW STRESSING ABOUT THE BOOBAGE IS TIME WASTED AND WHEN I'M AT MY PINK THINKING BEST, I TOTALLY LAUGH ABOUT HOW SILLY I'M BEING. BUT THERE ARE TIMES WHEN I SEE HOW EVA SATINE FILLS OUT HER RIDICULOUSLY EXPENSIVE TIGHT TEE AND I GET A SERIOUS TOUCH OF THE ENVY GREENS AND STUFF MY BRA WITH TOILET TISSUE IN THE HOPE I MIGHT LOOK NEARLY AS GOOD.

THING IS IT ITCHES REALLY BAD AND I'M SUPER-SCARED THAT IT'LL FALL OUT IN PUBLIC — HOW EMBARRASSING WOULD THAT BE?

IT'S THE SAME WHEN I WATCH MARILYN MONROE. I HEART HER. I HEART HOW HER CURVES FILL THE ENTIRE SCREEN. THEN I TAKE A LOOK AT MY TEENY-TINY BODY FRAME AND REALISE I DON'T HAVE CURVES. MORE SPECIFICALLY, I DON'T HAVE LADYBUMPS.

BUT I DO HAVE A GREAT COLLECTION OF FABULOUS CHILDREN'S SIZED TEES THAT I JUST COULDN'T WEAR IF I HAD LADYBUMPS. I ALSO KNOW THAT GORGEOUS GIRL BELLA DIDN'T GET HER BREASTICULARS UNTIL SHE WAS 16 AND BECAUSE SHE'S TALL AND SLENDER, THEY'RE PERKY AND PERT AND VERY DIFFERENT TO ANGEL WHO HAS MELON-LIKE BOOBS IN COMPARISON!

THE POINT IS, WE'RE ALL DIFFERENT SHAPES AND SIZES AND IT WOULD BE SUPER SILLY TO COMPARE MY BOOBAGE TO ANGEL, LOLA OR EVEN EVA, I'M REET PETITE AND AM NEVER GONNA HAVE KILLER GIRL-CURVES. THE GOOD NEWS IS, IT'S NOT WHAT'S IN MY TEE THAT DETERMINES IF I MEASURE UP, IT'S MY TOO-CUTE PERSONALITY AND ABILITY TO CUSTOMISE AN OUTFIT! RIGHT NOW, I'VE GOT BEE-STING LADYBUMPS, I SHALL LOVE THEM MOSTEST!"

Boobs: The Facts

Boobs are made up of fatty tissue and milk ducts. As you hit the big 'P' makeover, your nipples will start to change first and gradually you'll notice the area around the nipple getting bigger – these chica, are your boobs and they'll keep growing until you're about eighteen.

Don't stress if your ladybumps seem to be a different shape to those of your mates or if one of your boobs is slightly bigger than the other. Your body's still developing, so your shape will change a lot over the next few years, okay?

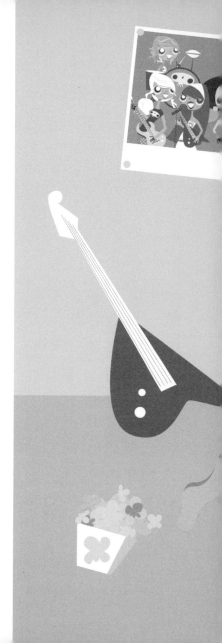

Boob worries, busted!

When do I need to get a bra?

As soon as you notice a change in shape, it's a good idea to consider a simple training bra, or sports bra. Most of these come in sizes of small, medium, and large. As your boobs get larger you will eventually need something with cups. Cups give you extra support and keep your breasts in place.

Why are mine different to everyone else's?

Every boob-bearing girl has worries about the shape and size of their ladybumps and it's common for girls to have one boob bigger than the other. Sometimes this sorts itself out as you get older, but most women will always have slightly different-shaped breasts and that's okay too. **Bod Squad tip:** If you feel uncomfy with un-even boobs, buy a padded bra and take the padding out of the side that's larger to even you out.

Help! I'm really flat chested!

Fear not – small boobs are totally normal. The hormones oestrogen and progesterone promote breast growth, so your boobs still have time to grow. But by the time you hit 20 they'll stay about the same size unless you put on or lose weight. Look at your mum and sister's chest size to get an idea of what's in store.

Bod Squad tip: Remember, we're all different shapes and sizes and that's such a good thing – a well-fitted bra will help enhance your shape and make you feel mucho confident.

My nipples look weird. Why?

Nipples come in all shape, colours and sizes. Some point inwards, some upwards and others to the left and right! Some girls have inverted nipples and this is also normal. Don't panic if you have hairs around your nipples either. This is not unusual and they can be painfully plucked away with tweezers if they really bother you.

Measure up!

Do your breasts show through your tee? Do they feel sore or uncomfy when you're playing sport? Basically, you wear a bra to be comfy, so if you think you'd be more comfortable with a bra than without, now is the time to get one!

Bella doesn't have a mum type so when it came to getting her first bra, she found it mucho difficult to ask her yoga-dad about it.

"...YOGA-DAD IS CHILLED ABOUT MOST THINGS, BUT COME ON, THIS WAS GIRL STUFF AND YOU CAN IMAGINE HOW EMBARRASSMONDO I FELT HAVING TO ASK HIM ABOUT BRAS. IT REALLY WAS NO BIGGIE THOUGH, SO DON'T STRESS. JUST LET YOUR PARENTALS KNOW THAT YOU'RE READY FOR A BRA. EXPLAIN WHY YOU THINK YOU NEED ONE — THEY'RE SORE, THEY WOBBLE WHEN YOU RUN, THEY SHOW THROUGH YOUR TOP — AND ASK IF THEY'LL HELP YOU SHOP FOR ONE..."

Right now, a massive 80% of UK chicas are wearing the wrong size bra – ouch! Wearing the right bra can make a big huge difference to your boob shape.

Bella sometimes found it hard to talk to her dad...

Ask yourself these questions:

Do your boobs spill out of the front or side of the bra?

Does your bra gradually ride up your back during the day?

Do the straps dig into your shoulder and leave red marks?

Can you see uneven lumps through your tops?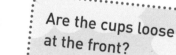

Are the cups loose at the front?

If you said yes to any of these, you need to get measured for a new bra, and should keep getting measured every 6 months as you grow and develop.

What's your bra size?

Before you buy a bra, I totally recommend you get measured up properly in a store like Marks and Spencers as they have lovely ladies who are trained specially to measure ladybumps! These fabulous ladies are called bra advisers, and they know their stuff. They will make sure your boobs are as comfy as possible. A bra advisor can help you make selections more quickly and can share her knowledge with you as well.

step 1	step 2 →									
	76 cm (25.5")	78 cm (30.5")	80 cm (30.1")	83 cm (30.5")	85 cm (33.0")	88 cm (34.5")	90 cm (35.0")	93 cm (36.5")	95 cm (37.0")	98 (38.
60 cm (23.5")	28AA	28A								
65 cm (25.5")		30AA	30A	30B	30C					
70 cm (27.5")				32AA	32A	32C	32D	32DD	32E	32
75 cm (29.5")					34AA	34A	34B	34C	34D	34[
80 cm (31.0")							36AA	36A	36B	36
85 cm (33.0")										38
90 cm (35.0")										
95 cm (37.0")										
110 cm 43.0")										

To get an idea of your size, follow the bod squad's 3 size-me-up steps:

- ☆ Measure directly under your boobs to get your rib size.
- ☆ Then measure around the fullest part of your boobs, over your nipples, to get your chest size. To find your size cross-reference these two measurements on the size-me-up chart.

100 cm (39.5")	103 cm (40.5")	105 cm (41.5")	108 cm (42.5")	110 cm (43.5")	113 cm (44.5")	115 cm (45.5")	118 cm (46.5")	120 cm (47.5")	123 cm (48.5")
32G									
34E									
36D	36DD	36E	36F	36G					
38B	38C	38C	38D	38DD	38E	38F	38G		
	40A	40B	40C	40D	40DD	40E	40F	40G	
			42A	42B	42C	42D	42DD	42E	42F
						44B	44C	44D	44DD

Blush-free bra shopping

The bod squad love to shop, and bra shopping is no exception!

★ Finding a bra that works for you takes a little more than snagging the first on the rail, so take your time, sweet thing!

★ Bra shopping should be fun, not embarrassing – think of your bra as a killer accessory – find one that works for you and deffo try before you buy!

★ Bras come in all shapes and sizes, styles and fabrics so here's our keep-'em-lookin'-fabulous guide to finding the bra for you!

Training bras – believe it or not chica, this bra isn't for training your ladybumps. Nope, it's for training you in the whole process that is bra-wearing! Even if you don't need the support just yet, wearing one can give you a confidence boost and make you feel less self-conscious when getting changed for PE or games!

Back hook and front hook bras – these pretty much do what they say on the label. They hook into place at the back/front with one or more tiny plastic/metal hooks. The back hook bras can take a bit of practice but it'll soon become as much a part of your mornin' routine as applying mascara in the hope that you'll get away with it at school.

Underwired bras – These have special wires sewn into the fabric that curve under your ladybumps for added support. If you have larger breasts, these can be fab to stop you from jiggling when you walk!

Padded bras – These bras have thicker, padded fabric to give the appearance of having larger boobs. Padded bras can be super tempting if you're impatiently waiting for your bee-stings to become ladybumps, but the chances are, you'll be much more comfy without the added padding. Try them, see what you think, but remember whatever size your boobs are, they're a part of what makes you totally you-nique so love them just as they are!

Sports bras – they look a lot like a cut-off vest top with a thick band of elastic at the bottom. They're designed to hold your boobs as-snug-as-a-bug-in-a-rug so they don't bounce around while you're being li'l miss work it girl!

Strapless bras – These bras stay on without straps and are perfect for when you wear tops or summer dresses without straps. They're sometimes not as comfy as regular bras, so save them for those days when you want to turn beach-girl and wear a too-cute strapless dress while playing Frisbee on the sand!

No matter what type of bra you choose – there are so many different kinds, in different colours and materials - have fun with it! The big 'P' makeover isn't all mucho serious-o y'know. Sure, you can be practical, but why not have a little fun with this growing up malarky too?!

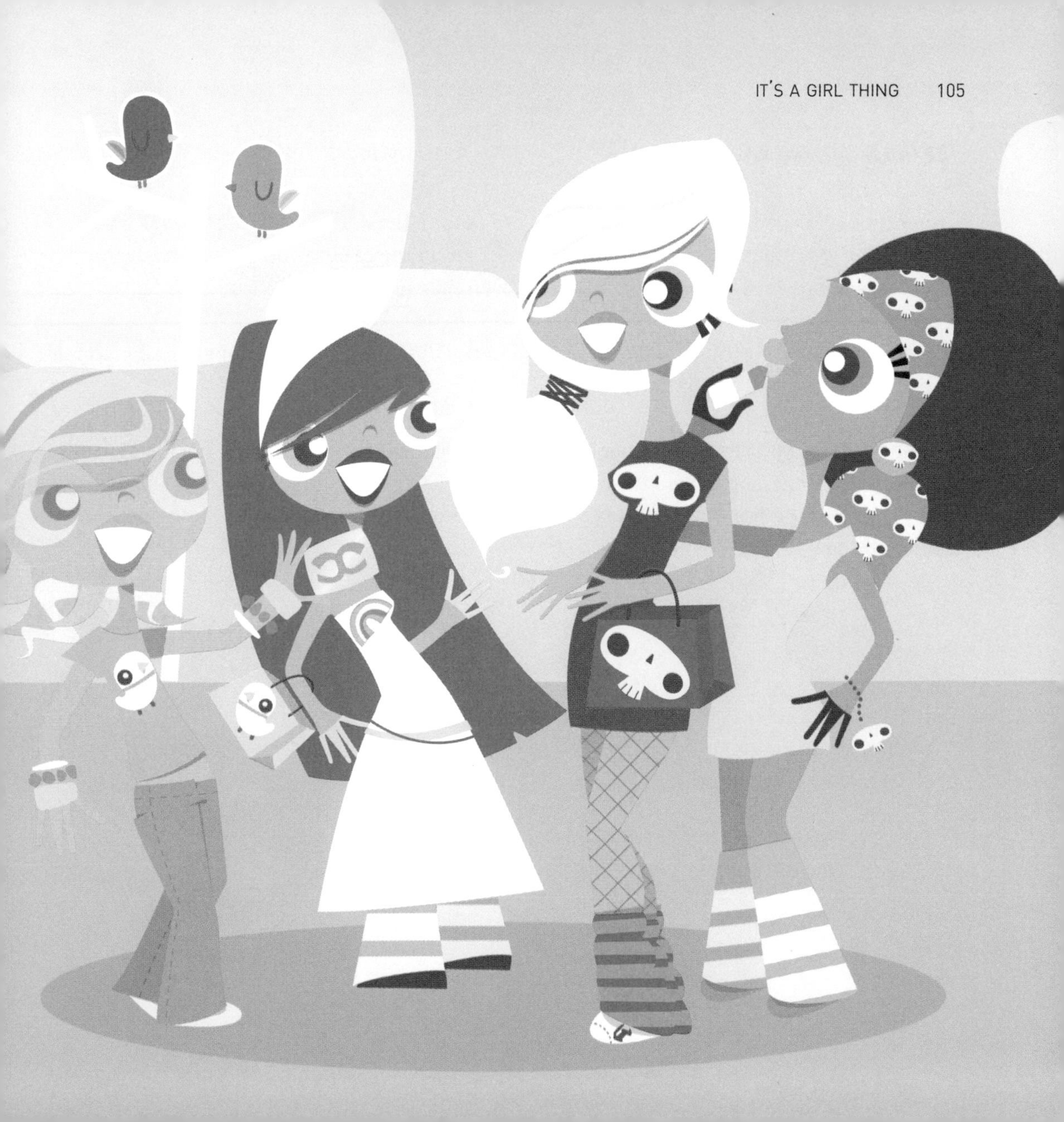

Work your ladybumps

The Pink Ladies and I know that our boobs are not the most important part of our sweet selves – no way – but super stylin' Angel does want to make sure you look as feisty, fun, fearless and fabulous with her 'work your ladybumps' dress code:

Big boobs: If you've got big boobs, V and scoop necklines, corset-style tops, fitted shirts and wrap dresses will all flatter your bust.

Small boobs: If you have small boobs then plump for halter necks, high neck t-shirts, chunky polo necks, and spaghetti straps. Any kind of extra detailing on the chest will look great. Never get a bra that's too big, or you'll end up with a tell-tale gap between your boob and the padding.

What you might notice about lads....

Girls aren't the only ones who go through changes during puberty, y'know. Yep, those boy types have their very own big 'P' makeover too. Well, it's only fair, isn't it?

We've called in the super cool Charlie, he's Angel's boy pal and although he's a boy, he hangs with us sometimes, knows Breakfast at Tiffany's word-for-word, and sings us tunes from our favourite musicals, which makes him pretty perfect in my book, and this is my book, right?!

So, Charlie, what's it like getting a boy version of the big 'P' makeover?

"OKAY GIRLS, SO YOU'LL BE PLEASED TO KNOW US BOYS GO THROUGH SOME PRETTY MAJOR CHANGES TOO AND, DUDE, SOME OF THEM AIN'T PRETTY... OUR ARMS, LEGS, HANDS AND FEET CAN GROW MUCH FASTER THAN THE REST OF OUR BODY, WHICH MEANS, UNTIL THE REST OF OUR BODY CATCHES UP, WE FEEL A LITTLE BIT CLUMSY.

WE GENERALLY GET TALLER AND OUR SHOULDERS WILL GET BROADER – THAT'S WHAT WE HOPE ANYWAY, BUT RIGHT NOW, IT'S NOT HAPPENING FAST ENOUGH IN CHARLIE WORLD - GRR.

THIS IS A MONDO BLUSH-INDUCING BIT — WE'LL ANSWER A QUESTION IN A CLASS, AND OUR VOICE WILL START CRACKING AND GO FROM HIGH-PITCHED TO A DEEP-DOWN-THERE VOICE — SO, SO EMBARRASSING. AS WE CONTINUE TO GROW, THOUGH, OUR VOICE WILL BECOME DEEPER AND STAY THAT WAY!

HAIR APPEARS UNDER OUR ARMS, ON OUR LEGS AND FACE, AND ABOVE OUR PENIS. CHEST HAIR MAY APPEAR DURING THE BIG 'P' MAKEOVER OR YEARS AFTER, ALTHOUGH NOT ALL MEN HAVE CHEST HAIR, I HAVEN'T AND HAVE TO SAY, I'M REALLY RATHER OKAY WITH IT!

OUR PENIS AND TESTICLES WILL GET LARGER — CANNOT BELIEVE I AM DISCUSSING THIS WITH YOU, GIRLS — AND WE MAY HAVE ERECTIONS (ERECTIONS OCCUR WHEN THE PENIS GETS HARD) SOMETIMES FOR NO REASON. THIS SOMETIMES MAKES A TROUSER-TENT, WHICH CAN CAUSE MAJOR EMBARRASSMENTO, ESPECIALLY IF IT HAPPENS IN PUBLIC — IT MAKES ME CRINGE JUST THINKING ABOUT IT!

ER, CAN I LEAVE NOW PLEASE? YOU'RE MAKING ME BLUSH!
SERIOUSLY, I'M NOT EMBARRASSED TO TALK ABOUT IT ALL, IT'S JUST MY BOY BOD TURNING INTO A MAN BOD, THAT'S ALL! THERE ARE, HOWEVER, A LOT OF BOYS WHO WILL BE EMBARRASSED OR SCARED ABOUT WHAT'S GOING ON, SO IF YOU NOTICE THEM ACTING A LI'L BIT WEIRD, BE SURE TO CUT THEM SOME SLACK AS THEY'RE MUCHO NERVY ABOUT THEIR BIG 'P' MAKEOVER TOO!"

Banish the blush

I hate blushing.

If ever I find myself in a sitch where I'd like the ground to swallow me up whole, I blush. In fact, blushing is like a neon-sparkly sign that flashes without my permission.

Rude.

So, why do our cheeks go red, exactly?

Well, when we're faced with something that might make us potentially blush-worthy, like, bumping into our cutester crush or speaking in front of the whole class, our bods don't know whether to see it through or leave quick-smart. So to try and get us moving, blood rushes to our muscles to make them faster and stronger. Some of this blood goes to our face and that, chica, is why we turn tomato red.

Like I said, rude.

What makes you blushsome?

....

....

....

....

....

....

....

....

....

....

....

....

....

....

If, like me, you suffer from the blushes, banish the embarrassment-o with these bod squad tips...

Stay calm – when your cheeks threaten an attack of the 'hot reds', breathe big, deep breaths and whatever the situation, don't stress. If you find yourself in a blush-worthy sitch - just chill.

Laugh it up – So what if you broke the chair in the science lab? So what if you accidentally said a rude word in a class presentation? Just shrug your shoulders and laugh it up, because when you laugh, chica, the world laughs with you!

Don't think about it – next time you feel your cheeks burning up, switch your thoughts to something totally dullsville instead, like a math sum or your geography homework. Before you know it, your blushes will have totally faded.

Be distract-o girl – The next time you find yourself feeling mucho embarrassmondo, distract the people you're with by changing the subject. If everyone sees you acting like you're not bothered, well they they won't care either – hurrah!

Cringe!

My most cringe-worthy moment-o ever has to be when I was invited to a fancy dress party. I was so excited, I love, love, love dressing up!

Except, I didn't receive the text. The text that said **"Lola, we're not doing dressing up anymore 'k?"** I arrived at the venue, working my best witch's costume – very Wicked-esque - warts and all, to be greeted by a swarm of bemused, sniggering faces.

Total mortification.

At the time, I wanted to run home and go dive under the duvet for quite possibly the rest of my life. I mean, what would they say at school the next day?

I would be the talk of the class, and not in a good way. Thing is, when you Think Pink, you work a sitch like this to your total advantage. Y'see, if it were to happen now, I would just take a big, deep breath and rock the evening out in my costume.

Oh, Gosh!

I would, y'know.

Because that way, I would be in control.

People would laugh with me if I was having a good time and if people were talking about me the next day, it would be because I was telling the story!

What's the most cringe-worthy thing to ever have happened to you?

....

....

....

....

....

....

....

....

....

How did you deal with it?

....

....

....

....

....

....

....

....

....

....

....

....

....

....

Deal with the Cringe

Smile – So what if you got your hair stuck in the zipper of a top in the changing room? So what if the snotty assistant had to help you out? Chica, you've got to laugh about it – because when you laugh, the world will laugh with you and there is nothing more attractive than a chica who knows how to laugh.

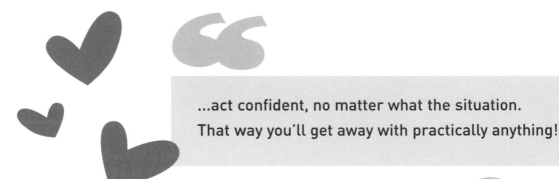

...act confident, no matter what the situation.
That way you'll get away with practically anything!

Fact.

Act up – If you trip over your words when talking to the cutester in your maths class or find yourself wearing the exact same outfit as your bestie – don't panic, just stand tall and ask yourself what your most favourite inspir-o girl would do – if ever I find myself in a tricky sitch, I'll say: "WHAT WOULD AUDREY DO?"

In most cases, she would be mucho chic and brush off any feelings of embarrasmento, pronto. So, make like Audrey, and act confident, no matter what the situation. That way you'll get away with practically anything!

Be silly – Chica, don't take yourself too seriously. Okay, so you've walked into class and your skirt is tucked in your Paul Frank knickers, instead of running in the opposite direction, simply throw your classmates a cheeky wink and do a li'l happy dance.
Oh, and then un-tuck them, obviously.

Love yourself up - If you're still cringing from the shame of letting out a bottom burp in front of your best bud and her family – don't.

Beating yourself up about it is gonna get you nowhere, so just forget about it! Instead, collect compliments - write 'em down in a cute li'l journal and you can flick back anytime you need to remind yourself how totally fabulous you are.

Think Pink! – If, after an embarrassmondo incident you're thinking: "WHAT A TOTAL IDIOT, JEEZ, I'M SO DUMB!" flick your negative switch to 'pink' and say this instead: "IT COULD HAVE BEEN A WHOLE LOT WORSE, IT'S NOT SUCH A BIG DEAL!"

It's a wrap!

Chica, I cannot deny that this growing up lark is a total exciting and scary rollercoaster ride and there will be times when your pink thinkin' beauty*liciousness will be tested by something as small as a pimple on your chin or as huge as a killer mood swing. At times like these, remember that you're a totally YOU-nique feisty, fun, fearless and fabulous Pink Lady who:

☆ Takes charge of your body by continuing to learn all you can about your sweet self; after all, it's your body, so it should be your specialist subject, right?

☆ Reap the benefits of a healthy self – and know that you're the one who has to deal with the consequences of bad decisions.

☆ Asks questions about what's going on with your bod – how else are you to become as feisty, fun, fearless and fabulous as you can possibly be?

☆ Tell your doctor/parentals about your concerns – without being embarrassed.

Chica, you're a super-sparkly girl of fabulousness!
Love and matching pink underwear...

Lola
xx

Lolo Love

The go for it girl's guide to life!

think pink
By Lisa Clark

The ultimate 'go-for-it' guide for girls!

Everything you need to know to live life like a star!

Viva la Diva
By Lisa Clark

Everything you need to know about being fabulous!

Beauty*licious
By Lisa Clark

The essential beauty bible starring **Lolo Love**

The essential beauty bible

Also starring Lola Love and the Pink Ladies...